HALL, Margaret

The life of William Wrigley, Jr.

The Life of
William Wrigley Jr.
and the story of Wrigley's chewing gum

M.C. Hall

First published in Great Britain by Heinemann Library, Halley Court, Jordan Hill, Oxford OX2 8EJ, part of Harcourt Education.
Heinemann is a registered trademark of Harcourt Education Ltd.

Editorial: Traci Todd and Harriet Milles
Design: Richard Parker and Maverick Design
Picture Research: Julie Laffin
Production: Camilla Smith

Originated by Repro Multi-Warna
Printed and bound in China by
South China Printing Company

The paper used to print this book comes from sustainable resources.

ISBN 0 431 18101 2
09 08 07 06 05
10 9 8 7 6 5 4 3 2 1

British Library Cataloguing in Publication Data
M.C. Hall
William Wrigley Jr. – (The Life of)
338. 7'6646'092
A full catalogue record for this book is available from the British Library.

Acknowledgements
The Publishers would like to thank the following for permission to reproduce photographs:
p. **4** Andrew E. Cook; pp. **5**, **11**, **21** Catalina Island Museum; p. **6** Hulton Archive/Getty Images; p. **7** Museum of the City of New York/Corbis; pp. **8**, **23** Hulton Archive/Getty Images; p. **9** Bettmann/Corbis; pp. **10**, **17** William Wrigley, Jr. Company; pp. **12**, **24** Corbis; pp. **13**, **14, 15** Mary Evans Picture Library; p. **16** Kit Kittle/Corbis; p. **18** Richard Cummins/Corbis; p. **19** Underwood & Underwood/Corbis; p. **20** Macduff Everton/Corbis; p. **22** Dallas and John Heaton/Corbis; p. **25** Wrigley Mansion Club Archives; p. **26** Janet Lankford Moran/Heinemann Library; p. **27** © Peter Jordan Photography

Cover photograph by The Granger Collection, Cover and interior icons Janet Lankford Moran/Heinemann Library

Contents

Words shown in the text in bold, **like this**, are explained in the Glossary.

A sticky treat

People have been chewing gum for thousands of years. For a long time, chewing gum was made from things like **sap** and wax. It did not always taste nice!

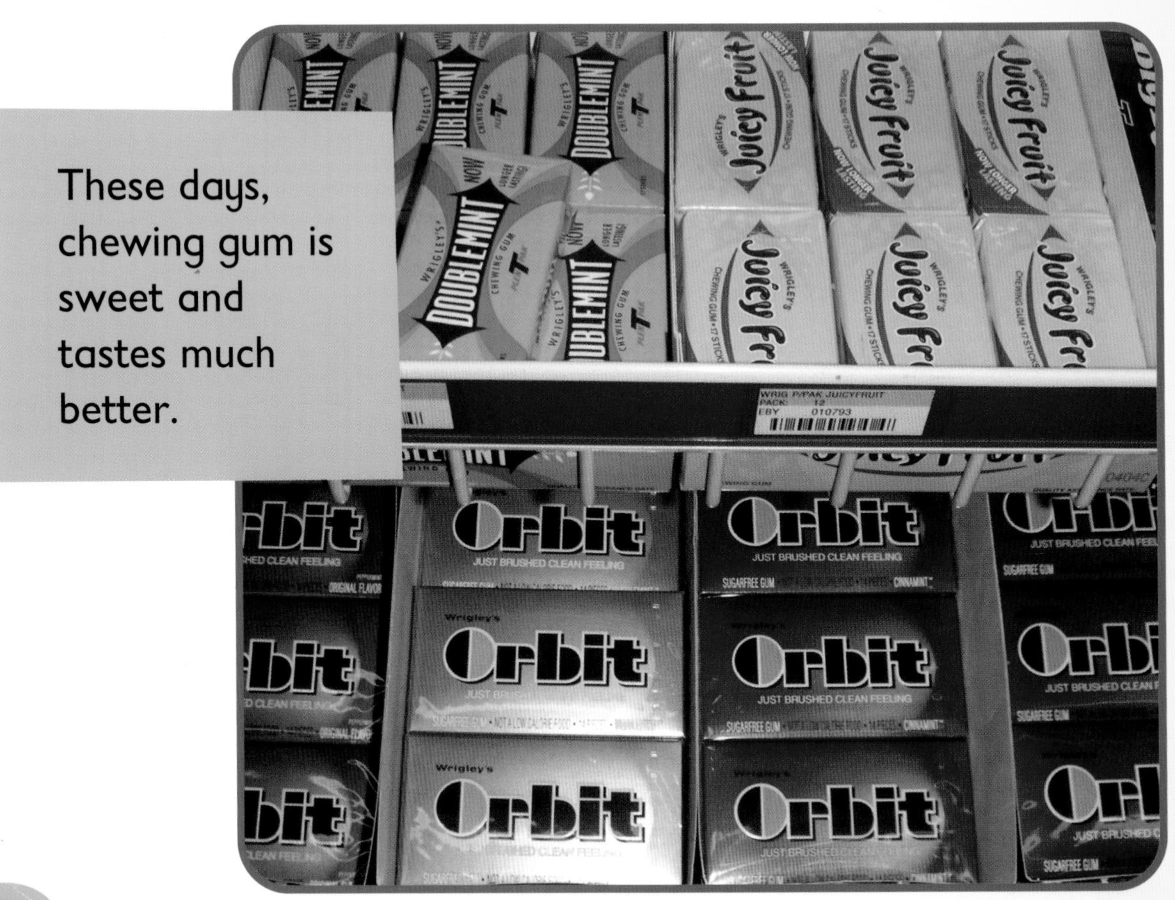

These days, chewing gum is sweet and tastes much better.

William Wrigley Jr. was good at selling things. At first he sold other people's **products**. Then he started one of the biggest chewing gum **companies** in the world.

This is William Wrigley Jr. in 1919.

The early years

William Wrigley Jr. was born on 30 September 1861, in Philadelphia, Pennsylvania, USA. He was one of nine children. William's father owned a soap **factory**.

This painting shows Philadelphia in the 1860s.

Newspaper boys sold newspapers on the streets.

When William was 11 years old, he ran away from home. He sold newspapers to earn money, and slept on the streets. When winter came, William went back home.

At work in the factory

William went back to school, but he soon got into trouble. The school threw him out. William's father was angry. He made William work in his soap **factory**.

At that time, there were many factories that made soap.

In the early 1900s, many children had to work in factories. Life was often hard for them.

William's father gave him one of the worst jobs in the factory. He had to stir large pots of boiling soap. William wanted to sell soap, not make it.

Selling soap

When William was 13 years old, his father agreed to let him sell soap. William became a **salesman**. He travelled long distances by horse and cart to visit his **customers**.

This is what Wrigley's soap looked like when William was selling it.

William did well and found new customers for his father's soap. In 1885, he married Ada Foote. William and Ada had two children. The family moved to Chicago, in 1891.

This is Ada when she was older.

Changing products

William had an idea to sell more soap. He gave free **baking powder** to **customers**. Soon people wanted to buy baking powder more than they wanted to buy soap!

William started selling baking powder.

William liked the idea of giving something away. He gave two packets of chewing gum to anyone who bought his baking powder. People wanted more gum. William decided to sell chewing gum.

This is an **advertisement** for chewing gum in the 1920s.

On his own

In the USA, there were already some **companies** that sold chewing gum. One of the largest companies offered William a job. William said no. He wanted to work on his own.

William wanted to sell chewing gum in many different flavours.

This is an **advertisement** from the 1930s for Wrigley's *Double Mint* gum.

William did not make the chewing gum himself. Instead, he paid another company to make his **products**. However, William's name was put on every packet of gum.

Prizes for buyers

Shopkeepers who sold Wrigley's gum were given prizes. They could choose from things like clocks, flags, pens, and cameras. This made the shopkeepers sell more gum.

This is an American shop in the early 1900s. William sold his chewing gum in places like this.

People started to ask for Wrigley's chewing gum by name. In 1911, William bought the **company** that made his gum. He gave it a new name – the William Wrigley Jr. Company.

Wrigley's Mile-Long sign **advertises** Wrigley's gum beside a railway line.

A growing business

William's **company** did very well and he became rich. He liked to buy things that interested him. In 1915, William gave money to the Chicago Cubs **baseball** team.

This is Wrigley Field where the Chicago Cubs play. It was called after William Wrigley in 1926.

This is a picture of baseball fans welcoming the Chicago Cubs to Catalina Island in 1930.

In 1919 William bought Catalina Island, off the coast of California. He built a baseball field there. The Chicago Cubs sometimes used this field for practice.

Catalina Island

William spent a lot of money **improving** Catalina Island. He paid to build roads, hotels, and water pipes. He also bought two large ships. He sold tickets so that people could visit the island on the ships.

Today, Catalina Island is a very popular place to go for a holiday.

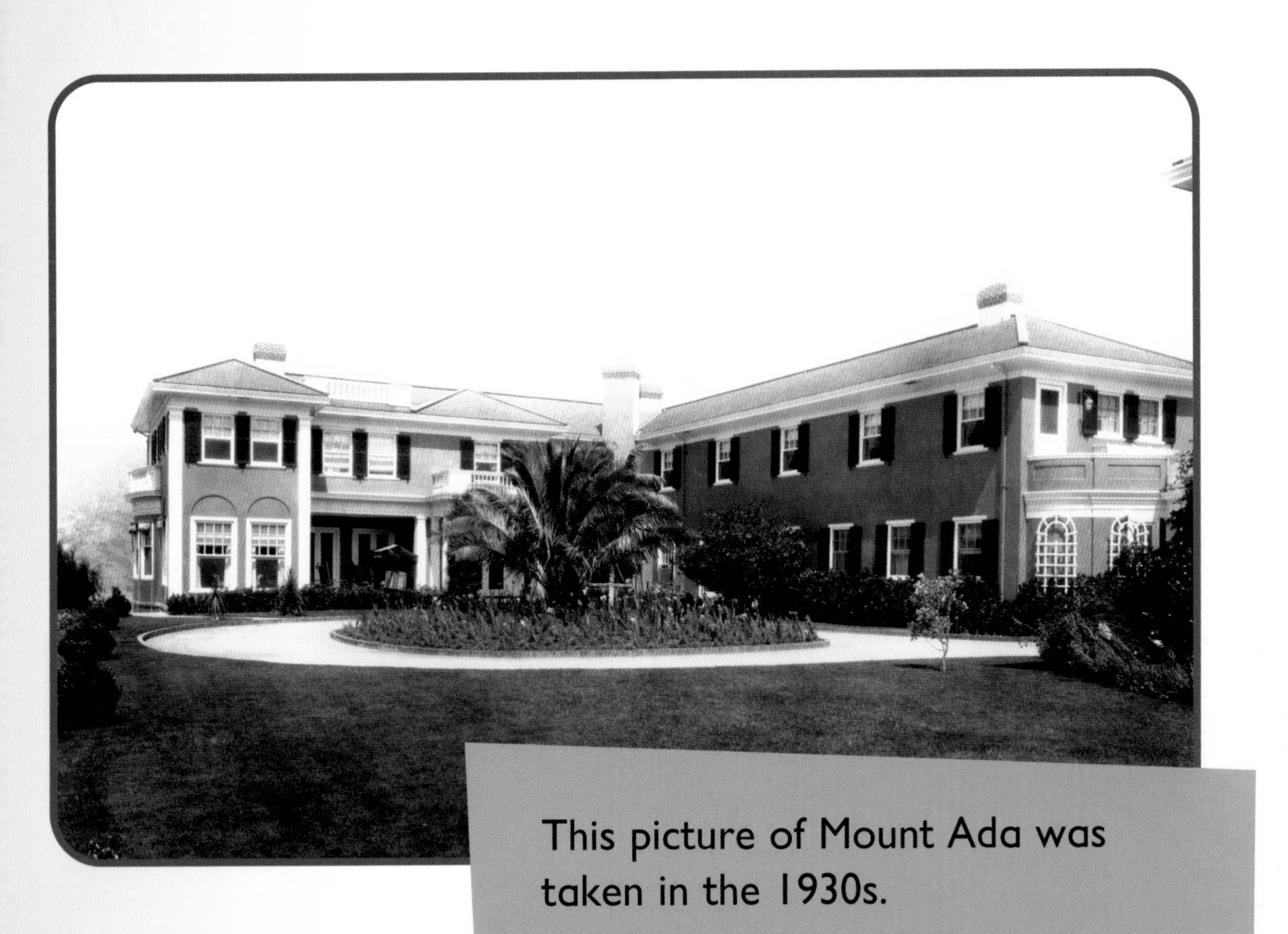

This picture of Mount Ada was taken in the 1930s.

William built a big house on Catalina Island. He called the house Mount Ada, after his wife. The Wrigleys stayed in this house when they visited the island.

The Wrigley Building

In 1920, William built a new building in Chicago for his **company**. At that time, the Wrigley Building was one of the tallest in the city. It was different because it was shaped like a triangle.

The Wrigley Building still stands in Chicago.

William Wrigley's son, Philip, started to run the company in 1925.

William ran the company for another five years. By then, the William Wrigley Jr. Company had **factories** in the USA, Canada, and Australia.

The later years

William and Ada spent part of each winter in Phoenix, Arizona. In 1929, William built a big house there. It was a 50th wedding anniversary present for Ada.

Here are William and Ada in 1929.

The Wrigley **Mansion** was huge. William owned four other houses that were even bigger. He and Ada only used the Phoenix house for a few months in each year.

The Wrigley Mansion in Phoenix had 12 bathrooms and 11 fireplaces!

More about William

William Wrigley Jr. died in Phoenix, Arizona on 26 January 1932. His grave is in Glendale, California. Today, his **company headquarters** is still in Chicago.

William Wrigley's chewing gum is still popular all over the world.

This is the Wrigley Mansion Club in Phoenix.

People can learn more about William by visiting the Wrigley **Mansion** in Phoenix. The house is now a club. Members pay ten US dollars a year. The money helps local people and groups.

Fact file

- When William first went to Chicago, he only had 32 US dollars. Later, he was a rich man. A packet of Wrigley's chewing gum only cost five US cents, but the **company** made millions of dollars.
- In 1924, the William Wrigley Jr. Company was the first to give all its workers Saturdays off.
- The William Wrigley Jr. Company is still owned by the Wrigley family. William's great-grandson is now company **president**.

Timeline

1861 William Wrigley Jr. is born in Philadelphia, Pennsylvania

1873 William starts to work in his father's soap **factory**

1874 William becomes a travelling **salesman**

1885 William marries Ada Foote

1891 William moves to Chicago, Illinois

1911 William buys the company that makes his chewing gum. He changes its name to the William Wrigley Jr. Company.

1919 William buys Catalina Island

1920 Work begins to build the Wrigley Building in Chicago

1925 William's son, Philip, takes over the running of the company

1926 The Chicago **baseball** park where the Chicago Cubs team play is given the name 'Wrigley Field'

1932 William Wrigley Jr. dies in Phoenix, Arizona

Glossary

advertise show or tell people about something they can buy

baking powder white powder used in baking and cooking

baseball American ball game, played by two teams, using a bat and a ball

company group of people who makes money by selling things

customers people who buy a product

factory building in which things are made

headquarters place from which a business is run

improving making something better

mansion very large house

president person in charge of running a company or a country

product something that is made

salesman man who sells things to other people

sap liquid found inside trees and other plants

Find out more

Books

Chewing Gum: A Sticky Treat, Elaine Landau (Rourke Publishing, 2001)

William Wrigley, Jr.: Chewing Gum Giant, Carole Marsh (Gallopade International, 1998)

Websites

www.wrigley.co.uk
Visit Wrigley's website to find out more about the company.

Index

Titles in *The Life of* series include:

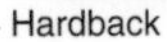
Hardback 0 431 18073 3

Hardback 0 431 18105 5

Hardback 0 431 18098 9

Hardback 0 431 18099 7

Hardback 0 431 18071 7

Hardback 0 431 18072 5

Hardback 0 431 18100 4

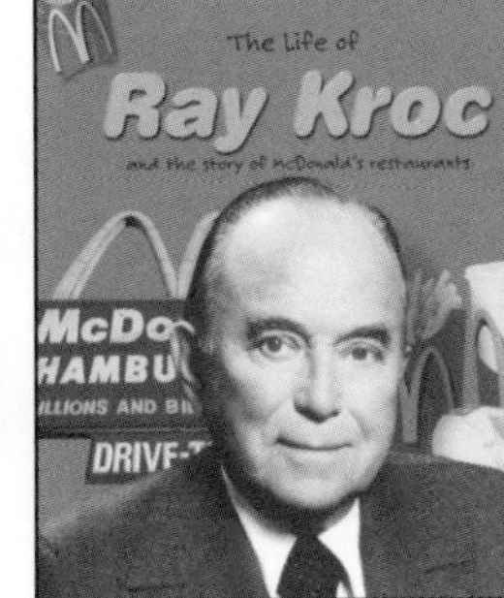

Hardback 0 431 18106 3

Hardback 0 431 18070 9

Hardback 0 431 18101 2

Find out about the other titles in the Heinemann Library on our website www.heinemann.co.uk/library